Breaking the Willow

Breaking the Willow

Poems of Parting, Separation and Reunion

Translated by David Lunde

Companions for the Journey Volume 18

White Pine Press / Buffalo, New York

Publication of this book was made possible, in part, with public funds from the New York State Council on the Arts, a State Agency.

Acknowledgments: Grateful acknowledgment is made to the editors of the following publications in which many of these translations first appeared:
Blue Unicorn: Du Fu, "Spring Outlook."
The Book Press: Bai Juyi, "Invitation to Liu Nineteen"; Du Fu, "On His Sad Departure from Changan by the Gate of Golden Light."
Borderlands: Liu Yong, "A Song of Parting."
Calapooya Collage: Du Fu, "Quatrain," "Thinking of My Brothers on a Moonlit Night," "Welcoming a Guest"; Li Bai, "Thinking of Her Husband in Spring."
Chaminade Literary Review: Du Fu, "Moonlit Night"; Li Bai, "Drinking Alone Beneath the Moon"; Li Shangyin, "Untitled."
Chelsea: Du Fu, "On Yueyang Tower," "Written While Traveling at Night"
The Cream City Review: Liu Zhi, "Song of Departure."
Acknowledgements continue on page 91.

Printed and bound in the United States of America.

First Edition

Cover: Detail from a painting by Yang Yongqing

Library of Congress Control Number: 2008928427

ISBN: 978-1-893996-95-3

White Pine Press, P.O. Box 236, Buffalo, New York 14201
www.whitepine.org

Contents

Foreword

I first began thinking about the importance of translation as an undergraduate English major, when we read Ezra Pound's translation of Li Bai's (Li Po, in the Wade-Giles system) "The River Merchant's Wife: A Letter." The poem stunned me. From the opening lines,

> While my hair was still cut straight across my forehead,
> I played about the front gate, pulling flowers.
> You came by on bamboo stilts, playing horse,
> You walked about my seat, playing with blue plums.
> And we went on living in the village of Chokan:
> Two small people, without dislike or suspicion.

which immediately pull the reader into the scene, establishing with concrete details the age of the children, their innocence, the peace of the village, the boy's interest in the speaker, we know that their relationship is going to deepen as they get older. Pound's marvelous translation is like time travel, bringing the lives of an 8th century Chinese village so vibrantly into our present that we feel we know these people. I think that this translation is one of the finest poems in English of the 20th century. And here's the thing that struck me beyond the poem itself: Pound did not know Chinese! He was working from the notes and literal renderings left by the scholar Ernest Fenollosa, whose widow had asked Pound to make translations from them. Pound's own understanding as a poet had allowed him to recreate Li Bai's poem in a new language in a new century and "make it new" in his own phrase.

This stuck in my mind, though it would be thirty years before I actually attempted to follow Pound's example in translating Chinese poetry. At that time I was just beginning to write poetry of my own, and that was challenge enough.

Then, fifteen years ago now, my friend and colleague George Sebouhian, who had recently returned from a Fulbright Fellowship spent in Japan, made a presentation to the English Department on Japanese poetry, specifically a five line poem by the mid-9th century poet Ono no Komachi. The poem was shown in Japanese characters, then in English transliteration, followed by a literal word for character translation which included the various possible meanings of the characters. Then he showed us three published

English translations, none of which seemed to have successfully captured the feeling of the original, and two of which were ludicrously bad. Naturally, being a poet myself, I couldn't resist attempting to do it better, and I gave it a try. When George saw how interested I was, he introduced me to a fascinating small book called *Nineteen Ways of Looking at Wang Wei* by Eliot Weinberger and Octavio Paz, the Nobel Prize-winning Mexican poet.

This book presents a quatrain by the Tang Dynasty poet Wang Wei in the same way that George had presented the Ono no Komachi poem, but in this case there are nineteen translations, sixteen into English, two into French and one into Spanish. They range over the span of time from W.J.B. Fletcher's 1919 rendition to that of Gary Snyder in 1978. Each is astutely—and sometimes caustically—commented upon by Paz and Weinberger.

What struck me most powerfully about this, was the degree to which the effect of the poem on the reader varied from version to version, and how greatly one's understanding of it was in the hands of the translator. And obviously in many cases one was in very bad hands.

I suppose this should not have come as much of a surprise to me, since I had taken a translation workshop in graduate school at the University of Iowa Writers' Workshop and had been translating French poetry, and occasional poems from other Romance languages, for twenty-five years. However, for the most part, I had been translating modern and contemporary French poets. I knew that the modern poets had all been very well translated by others, but I made translations of some of their poems, without reading other translators' versions, then compared them, just for practice. The contemporary poets had mostly been little translated, so there wasn't much to compare mine with, but my teachers approved them and many were published. After leaving Iowa and obtaining a teaching job at the State University of New York at Fredonia, I continued to make translations of contemporary French poets, as well as much older work by François Villon and the Provençal troubadour poets. I also collaborated with a colleague in the Foreign Language department, Frank Capozzi, in translating a collection of selected poems by the Italian poet Pier Paolo Pasolini.

But I had never made the kind of comparative study of translations that Weinberger and Paz had, and I wondered if the translators of other Chinese poetry had gone as far off track as many of those who attempted the Wang Wei poem had. I began collecting and comparing translations of classical Chinese poetry and quickly found that they varied enormously in style, tone, word choice, and general readability. Some were simply paraphrases focused on explaining the poem, rather than recreating it in a new language, which is fine if one is a student wanting to know 'what the poem is about', but not at all fine if one wishes to experience it as a poem.

These translations fell into two general categories: poems translated by scholars, and poems translated by poets. The translations by scholars, even when they were presented in lines as if they were poetry, tended to wordiness and awkwardness, and paid little or no attention to rhythm or sound. Poets, on the other hand, sometimes took great liberties with the original in both form and content, some seeming to use the original merely as a starting point for their own poem.

There was no way to judge just how well or poorly these translators had done, however, without knowing exactly what the original poet had written. What I needed were literal word-for-character translations made by knowledgeable scholars, and commentaries on the poems and the poets, and their historical and cultural contexts. Luckily, for many of the most prominent poets, this information was available in university libraries, and I began accumulating as much as I could.

From then on, I made translations based on my understanding of the original texts in light of the commentaries and other versions. Having been encouraged by success in publishing translations from other languages, I hoped that I could do better by the poets than others had by sticking as close to my sense of the original as possible and using what skills I had as a poet to make them read as satisfactory poems in English. However, the gap between modern English poetry and the language and culture of ancient China is much greater than that between English and the Romance languages and cultures, and I approached the translation of these poems with some trepidation.

Nonetheless, when I had accumulated a number that I was pleased with, I began sending them to literary magazines and found that there was a ready market (the word market is used with some irony here, as one seldom receives payment for poems) for them. Naturally, I was pleased, but I still had no idea how accurate my translations were, as it was unlikely that the editors of these magazines had any great knowledge of Chinese poetry. At that point I determined to send some to a magazine whose editors were experts. The magazine I chose, *Renditions: A Chinese-English Translation Magazine,* which was published by the Research Centre for Translation at the Chinese University of Hong Kong, seemed ideal: they could be expected to give my work a critical reading if anyone could. Once the poems were in the mail, I waited nervously for the response.

In the meantime, I had sent a group of translations to the *The Carolina Quarterly.* The editor passed them along to Professor J.P. Seaton of the Asian Studies Department for evaluation. Professor Seaton is a well-known scholar and translator of Chinese poetry, and it was a thrill for me to receive his letter in which he said that although he had advised the magazine not to use my translations because they were of poems that had been often translated and published previously, he did think they were well done. He subsequently aided me in publishing a number of other translations in *The Literary Review,* but more importantly we have kept in touch ever since, and his support and encouragement have meant a great deal to me.

Then I received the response from *Renditions.* The editor, Dr. Eva Hung, called my translations "highly polished and communicative," and she tentatively accepted two, pending their evaluation by a referee. The most astonishing thing, though, was her final statement: "I and my colleagues are curious about your background because the translations are very well done. Did you study Chinese formally?" Then I had to tell her the things I've just been telling you.

Dr. Hung has continued to be a supporter of my work by publishing it in her magazine over the years, but much more importantly, she has made it possible for me to work directly with Chinese scholars in translating both ancient and modern poetry. When Dr. Alice Cheang asked her to recommend translators to work on a projected anthology of Song Dynasty poetry to be titled *A Silver Treasury of Chinese Lyrics,* I was one of those recommended. Dr. Cheang, in turn, connected me with two of the scholars working on the anthology, Professors Mary M.Y. Fung and Teresa Yu. My collaborations with both of these fine scholars were not only successful, but educational and very enjoyable, and we have developed lasting friendships. I now feel quite secure in my translating, as I have several experts who won't hesitate to point out my errors.

Professor Fung and I entered into another collaboration the next year, translating the collected poems of the 20th century Chinese poet, Bian Zhilin. Our book, *The Carving of Insects,* to our great astonishment and joy, won the 2007 PEN U.S.A. Translation Award.

—David Lunde
May 2008

Introduction: Bureaucracy Saves Poetry

Unlike most peoples, the Chinese have no early creation myth, nor any legend of a migration to China from some other part of the world. As far as they are concerned, there have always been people like themselves living in this geographical area—originally Northern China near the Yellow River—and this belief seems to be borne out by the archaeological record. Skeletons of early hominids (*Pithecanthropus pekinensis*) have been found, dating from at least 200,000 BCE, which possess shovel-shaped incisors, a characteristic of present day Mongoloid peoples. Subsequently, neolithic civilizations developed which had settled villages, practiced agriculture, domesticated animals, made painted pottery, cast bronze, and used compound bows and chariots in warfare, among other arts of civilization.

For much of its history China was isolated from the rest of the world by its topology. As far as its inhabitants knew, there was only one sort of people in the world. All of the peoples living on its borders, although culturally, and some linguistically, different, were of the same Mongoloid stock. This may have contributed to their idea of an orderly universe, managed by a benevolent supreme being.

China was one of the few civilizations to independently develop writing. Although tradition ascribes its origin to the culture hero, Fu Hsi, some 1500 years earlier, its actual beginnings can be seen in the markings on Shang Dynasty oracle bones, some of which have been deciphered to yield tantalizing glimpses of the culture of that time. The importance of writing to the Chinese can be seen in their equivalent of the western term "civilization." Rather than focusing on learning to live together in cities, as this term does, the Chinese term *wen hua* means "the transforming influence of writing."[1] And of course they were correct: writing changes everything. It makes history possible: the knowledge of the past can be retained and built upon, rather than having to be rediscovered over and over—or lost forever. It drastically accelerates the development of science and technology. And, essential to our present purpose, it makes literature possible.

The basic texts of Chinese literature are the "Confucian Classics": the *I ching* (Book of Changes), which deals with the interpretation of divinations using oracle bones and tortoise shells; the *Shu ching* (Book of Writings), a collection of speeches, announcements, counsels, etc. made by rulers and their ministers in early times; the *Shih ching* (Book of Odes), a collection of 305 poems, which include folk songs, court songs, and ceremonial songs [it is this collection that is relevant to my book, as it is the foundation of later Chinese poetry]; the *Chun chiu* (Spring and Autumn Annals), a rather uninformative listing of historical and social events, i.e., "There was a great drought."; and the *Li* (Rituals), a collection of texts dealing with governmental organization, proper gentlemanly conduct, and the conduct of weddings, funerals and other ceremonies.

The compilation and editing of many of these works of antiquity, or parts of them, were attributed to Confucius (551–479 BCE) himself, who was a historian, scholar, and dedicated teacher, but while he probably had a hand in compiling and editing some of them, his actual contributions are uncertain. *The Book of Odes,* for instance, is thought to have been compiled by a group of scholars around 600 BCE. What is certain, however, is that Confucius drew upon these works for examples in his teachings, which dealt with proper conduct in all areas of life, from the duties of a ruler to his subjects, and theirs to him, and those of all the other levels of society down to those of the father to his wife and children and theirs to him. Confucius believed in an orderly heaven which had moral imperatives that people should follow in order to have peaceful and fulfilling lives. If a ruler, for example, mismanaged his kingdom and mistreated his subjects, heaven would cause him to be overthrown by a more righteous ruler. This doctrine was often applied retroactively to justify the overthrowing of a regime—if the usurper succeeded, then obviously the previous ruler had been at fault and deserved to have been deposed, and just as obviously, heaven was on the side of the conqueror. The Confucian principles have shaped the Chinese view of proper conduct and duties in all areas of life for the last two thousand years.

However, for our purposes, what is most important about Confucius is that "He and his school are responsible for the pedagogic tradition which characterizes all of later Chinese history, for the optimistic belief in the perfectibility of man through learning, and for the reverence for the scholar and the man of letters so pronounced in Chinese society."[2] No other country has so profoundly and consistently revered learning and teaching and writing.

Writing was put to work during the Ch'in Dynasty in the creation of China's second most important invention: bureaucracy, which though subject to the same inefficiencies and proliferation of unnecessary paperwork then as now, made possible a high degree of continuity throughout Chinese history, in spite of frequent political upheavals. The importance of this institution seems to be reflected in the Chinese concept of Heaven:

> Perhaps the most curious fact about the Chinese Pantheon is that it is arranged in imitation of earthly organization. It appears as a vast government administration, or still more precisely, as a series of government departments, each one with its Minister and its personnel. The different gods are

> positive bureaucrats with a strict hierarchy of rank and with clearly defined powers. They keep registers, make reports, issue directives, with a regard for formalities and a superabundance of papers which the most pedantic administration on earth might well envy.
>
> Every month they furnish a detailed report to their immediate superiors, and they every year give an account of their administration to the sovereign god, the August Personage of Jade, who then distributes his praise and his censure. The gods, according to circumstances, are then promoted or lowered in rank, and they may even be dismissed.
>
> This is one of the most original characteristics of all Chinese mythology, for the gods are not immutable. Only function persists–the functionary changes. New gods take the place of the old. And these changes do not only occur in time, but in space. By that we must understand that in different regions the same powers are in many instances allotted to quite a varying number of different personages.
>
> The explanation is that most Chinese gods are not in origin divine, but human; they are men who have been deified after their death."[3]

It seems most likely, therefore, that the Chinese idea of Heaven was formulated after the development of its earthly bureaucratic system, which was projected into it.

Bureaucracy itself became official policy under Emperor Wu of the Han Dynasty. His minister, Tung Chungshu, urged the Emperor to adopt Confucianism as the official state philosophy, and also to create a state university for the training of officials, who would be taught Confucian principles. All those who graduated would be assigned positions in the bureacracy. Along with this, a national civil service examination would be used to choose promising students. By the end of the Han period there were over 30,000 students enrolled in the university.

Why do I dwell on Chinese bureaucracy in a book of poetry? Because this bureaucracy and the mental outlook that went with it are responsible for having preserved China's literary tradition throughout its long history, and in spite of frequent and drastic changes of regime. The rise of this class of scholar officials led to typical scholarly hobbies such as collecting books, scrolls, paintings and other artworks. This in turn provided later scholars, down to our own time, with enormous quantities of source material for their own research and publications, and the duplication of texts, which was greatly facilitated by the invention of paper in the first century CE, and wood block printing, which was introduced during the Tang Dynasty, helped to ensure that works were not irretrievably lost. (Movable type was also invented first in China by Pi Sheng in 1041 CE, but was of little use because of the large number of characters in the Chinese language.)

Finally, the national civil service examinations, which all prospective bureaucrats (everyone who wanted to have a career) must pass, required a thorough knowledge of poetry, including the ability to write a poem in the style of a given famous poet of the past. Poetry had acquired high status because early interpreters of the *Book of Odes* had, quite mistakenly in the opinion of more recent scholars, drawn all sorts of moral lessons from it. The result was that all educated persons were familiar with poetry and wrote poetry themselves, at least occasionally. At social gatherings it was common for people to recite favorite poems (actually, they were sung, rather than recited as we do) and to compose poems extemporaneously, often on a theme or in a form suggested by one of the group.

Our society, unfortunately, has not yet reached such a high level of development, but I keep hoping.

—D. L.
May 2008

1 - Professor Derk Bodde, "Introduction to the History of China, " p. 10, in *China: A History in Art.* New York: Harper & Row, 1973.

2 - Wm. Theodore de Bary, Wing-tsit Chan, Burton Watson. *Source of Chinese Tradition.* New York and London: Columbia University Press, 1960.

3 - "Chinese Mythology" p. 380, in *New Larousse Encyclopedia of Mythology.* London, New York, Sydney, Toronto: The Hamlyn Publishing Group, Ltd., 1978.

This book is for J. P. "Sandy" Seaton
and
Eva Hung
who encouraged my early efforts at Chinese translation.

Breaking the Willow

In Chinese poetry, the willow is often associated with parting because in T'ang times it was a custom to break a willow twig and present it to a departing friend.

—James J.Y. Liu, *The Art of Chinese Poetry*

Anonymous

(from the *Book of Songs,* 12th c. b.c.e.–3rd c. b.c.e.)

Shijing 44

The two boys climbed into their boats,
whose shadows wavered beside them.
I think longingly of them,
heart trembling, their fate unclear.

The two boys climbed into their boats,
which drifted away on the stream.
I think longingly of them;
they've come to harm I fear.

Yuan Ji (210–263)

Insomnia

Unable to sleep in the depths of night,
I rise and sit to play the singing lute.
Through the thin curtains I see the bright moon;
a light breeze flutters my robe.
A solitary goose calls in the outer wilds;
circling birds cry in the northern woods.
Pacing back and forth, what do I hope to see?
Alone with my wounded heart, my empty longing.

Xie Lingyun (385–433)

Surveying My Fields, I Climb Mount Panxu at the Mouth of the Sea

What consolation is there for an exile's bitter sorrow?
I gaze at the sea, console myself with the dawn breeze.
No one can know the vast waves' limit;
no one can know the great deeps in the east.
I recall the lovely "Picking Water Chestnuts" song,
but for me it contains a scowling frown.
I ramble aimlessly over islands of jasper-green sand;
I wander on and on among peaks red as cinnabar.

Meng Haoran (689–740)

Poem Sent to Old Friends While Staying Overnight on the Donglu River

In these gloomy mountains I hear the sad calls of apes;
like the blue river, night flows in quickly.
Wind cries in the leaves of both riverbanks;
the moon shines down on my solitary boat.
Jiande county is not my home—
I remember old companions in Yangzhou city.
I write out two lines of tears
and send them far downstream to the west.

In the Twilight of the Year, I Return to the South

I give up petitioning the palace towers in the north;
I return to my poor cottage on South Mountain.
Saying I had no talent, the Shining Ruler cast me aside.
My illnesses are many, my friends scattered and few.
White hair makes plain my passing years;
spring drives the last of the old year away.
Depressed and brooding, I cannot sleep;
the moon shines through pines, but my window is empty.

Wang Changling (698–756)

Enjoying the Moonlight with My Cousin in the South Study and Thinking of Our Friend Cui in Shanyin

Relaxing on a seat in the south study,
we open the curtain just as the moon is rising.
Its pure light casts tree shadows on the water,
and their reflections dance in our room.
Full moon, then new, each in its turn
shining down now as it has in all ages.
Tonight you are beside a clear river
somewhere in Yue, singing sad songs.
A thousand miles apart, what else can we do?
A light breeze brings in a faint scent of orchids.

Wang Wei (701–761)

A Farewell

We dismounted, shared wine,
and I asked where you were off to.
"My dreams are shattered," you said,
"I'm retiring to South Mountain—
ask no more," and off you went.
White clouds drift on forever.

Farewell in the Mountains

Our farewells in the mountains are over;
With dusk coming on, I close my door.
Spring grass is green year after year,
But my friend I may see no more.

Seeing Yuan Second Off to An Xi

Morning rain wets the light dust in Wei city;
willows spring green, so green beside the guest house.
Let's drain another wine cup—
west of the Yang Pass no old friend awaits you.

Li Bai (701–762)

Seeing Meng Haoran Off to Yangzhou

From Yellow Crane Tower my old friend leaves;
in the third month flower-mists he heads down to Yangzhou.
Lonely sail, distant silhouette, gone into blue emptiness;
I see only the long river flowing to the edge of heaven.

Drinking Alone Beneath the Moon

One jar of wine among the flowers,
no dear friend to drink with:
I offer a cup to the moon.
With my shadow there are three of us,
but the moon doesn't know how to drink,
and my shadow can't help but follow me.
Still, I'll make do with their company,
have fun and make the most of spring.
I sing and the moon rolls around,
I dance and my shadow leaps about.
While I'm lively we enjoy each other,
when I get too drunk we go our own ways.
Let's keep this undemanding friendship
till we join together in the far Cloud River.

Sad Thoughts in Spring

In Yan, the grass is but green threads;
in Qin, the mulberry trees are thick with leaves.
By the time you turn your heart toward home,
my own will have already broken.
The spring wind and I no longer know each other:
why should it part my silk gauze curtain?

Seeing Off a Friend

Green mountains rise above the northern outskirts;
white water winds around the eastern city wall.
From this ground, once we say farewells,
like a tumbleweed you will roll a thousand miles.
Floating clouds are the wanderer's thoughts,
the sinking sun the feelings of his old friend.
With a wave of your hand you ride away;
our horses neigh at their separation.

Leaving Early from White Emperor City

We left White Emperor among dawn-reddened clouds.
A thousand miles to Jiangling, crossed in a day!
From both riverbanks, the constant shriek of gibbons;
already our small boat has passed a thousand serried
mountains.

Du Fu (712–770)

Moonlit Night

Tonight my wife must watch alone
the moon shining over Fuzhou;
I think sadly of my sons and daughters far away,
too young to understand my absence in Changan.
With fragrant mist, her cloud-like hair is damp;
in clear moonlight, her jade-white arms are cold.
When will we lean at the open casement together
while the moonlight dries our shining tears?

Spring Outlook

The nation is torn apart, but mountains and rivers remain;
it's spring in the city, grass and trees grow thick.
Feeling the times, flowers drip with tears;
seeing us parted, birds shriek heart-rending cries.
Soldiers' beacons have burned three months in a row;
I'd give ten thousand in gold for a letter from home.
I scratch my white hair shorter yet—
soon it will be too thin to hold a hairpin.

Beside Serpentine Lake

The old man from Shaoling
chokes back his sobs
wandering the bends of Serpentine
furtively on a spring day:

The riverside palaces
have locked their thousand doors;
for whom do the weeping willows
send forth their new green shoots?
I remember the Emperor's banner
like a rainbow over the Lotus Pool Garden,
and everything in the park
aflame with new color.
The First Lady of Zhaoyang palace
rode beside the Emperor in his carriage.
Maids of honor riding before
carried bows and arrows;
their white horses champed at golden bridles
as they bent back their bodies
and loosed arrows at the clouds.

The Lady laughed in delight
as one brought down flying wings.
The bright eyes, the gleaming teeth,
where are they now? Tainted with blood,
her wandering soul cannot return.
The Wei River flows eastward,
and Jiange Pass is far away.
He who left and she who stayed
can no longer exchange news.
It is only human to have feelings
and soak our bosoms with tears,
but the river's water and its flowers
never change and never care.
In the twilight the city is filled
with the dust of barbarian horsemen.
I want to go to the South City,
but my gaze keeps straying north.

On His Sad Departure from Changan by the Gate of Golden Light

This is the way I left before, to reach the Emperor's territory;
barbarians were everywhere in the western suburbs.
Until now I had not regained my courage;
the souls driven from my body must not have returned.
On his return to the capital, I was in the Emperor's
entourage—
surely it was not His Sacred Majesty who ordered my
demotion!
Judged incompetent, daily more old and decrepit,
I rein in my horse and gaze at the doors of the palace.

Missing Li Bai at the End of the Earth

A cold wind comes up, here at the end of the earth,
and I wonder what your intentions are—
when will my wild goose arrive at last?
Lakes and rivers are swollen this autumn.
Literature hates the writer who does too well;
mountain goblins eagerly await the traveler.
You ought to talk with the wronged ghost of Qu Yuan,
drop him a poem-offering into the Miluo River.

Dreaming of Li Bai (1)

Parting with the dead, one eventually stops sobbing,
but when parting with the living sorrow never ends.
You're exiled to Yelang in Jiangnan, place plagued by malaria,
and no news of you, old friend. But you enter my dream
tonight for you are always in my thoughts.
You are now tangled up in the nets of the law;
how did you free your wings to fly here?
It makes me fear this soul of yours is not of one still living.
The road between us is too long to measure.
When your soul came this way, you could see green maples,
but journeying back it will travel through dark passes.
As I wake, the sinking moon floods the roof-beams with
    light,
and I stare about, half-expecting it will shine on your face.
Between us the water is deep and the waves broad and tall—
don't let the water-dragons seize you, my friend!

Dreaming of Li Bai (2)

All day long clouds float restlessly,
still the wanderer does not arrive.
Three nights in a row I've dreamt of you:
I can see the kindly concern in your mind,
but you always leave in a rush,
saying ruefully, "Coming here wasn't easy—
the wind blows wild waves on river and lake;
I was afraid I'd lose my oars and capsize."
You go out the door scratching your white hair
as if disappointed in your life's dreams.
The capital city is filled with officials—
why should this man be made so wretched?
Who says the Emperor casts a wide net
in his search for men of talent?
Li is getting old, and still suffering in exile.
Making a name to last a thousand autumns
is a pointless post-mortem affair.

Thinking of My Brothers on a Moonlit Night

Garrison drums cut off travel.
It's fall; on the frontier a single wild goose calls.
From this night on, the dew will shine white;
the moon is bright, but not back-home bright.
I have younger brothers, all parted and scattered,
and no family left to ask if they live or die.
I send letters but they never arrive,
and it's worse as this war drags on and on.

Poem for Wei Ba

Often a man's life is such that he seldom sees his friends,
like the constellations Shen and Shang which never share
the same sky.
If not this evening, then what evening should we share this
lamp light?
How long can our youth and vigor last? The hair at our
temples is already gray.
We inquire about old acquaintances to find that half are
ghosts—
shocked cries betray the torment of our hearts.
How could I have known that it would be twenty years
before I again entered your honored home.
When we parted last you were yet unmarried;
now your sons and daughters line up in a smiling row
to greet their father's friend. They ask where I have come from,
but before I can answer all questions you chase them off
to bring wine and cups. In the night rain, chives are cut
for the freshly steamed rice mixed with yellow millet.
Saying how difficult it has been for us to meet at last,
you pour ten cups in a row! But even after ten cups
I'm not drunk, being so moved by your lasting friendship.
Tomorrow we will be separated by the peaks of mountains,
each of our worldly affairs lost to the other's sight.

Welcoming a Guest

Spring floods, both north and south of my house;
everywhere the flocks of gulls flying in day after day.
The flower-strewn path hasn't yet been swept for a visitor,
but today I open my wickerwork gate for you.
We'll make do with what's here—the market is too far.
Our home is poor, the wine in our bottle no longer fresh,
but if you are willing to drink with my old neighbor next
door,
I will call across the hedge and we'll share the last cups.

A Second Farewell to Governor Yen Wu at Fengji Post Station

We have come far together, but here we must part;
the green hills echo my feelings in vain.
When will we again take wine cups in hand
to stroll as we did beneath last night's moon?
Every district sings sad songs at your leaving;
three reigns now you have served with distinction.
Now I must go back to my river village alone,
and alone live out the rest of my days.

On Learning that Our Troops Have Retaken Henan and Hebei

Word from the front: our soldiers have retaken Hebei!
As soon as I hear this, my robe is soaked with tears.
I turn to look at my wife and children–where did our sorrow go?
I pack up my poems helter-skelter, so happy I'm witless.
Broad day, and I'm singing aloud–it's time for some wine!
With green spring for company, what a joyful trip home!
I will go straight from Ba Gorge down through Wu Gorge,
then on to Xiangyang and home, home to Luoyang!

Quatrain

Birds gleam white on the blue river,
mountains are deep green, flowers in full blaze.
Look! once again, spring is gone—
what day, what year, will I return home?

Passing the Night at Headquarters

Clear autumn at headquarters, wutung trees cold by the well;
I spend the night alone in the river city, burning my candle
down.
Sad bugle notes sound through the long night as I mutter
to myself;
glorious moon hanging in mid-sky but who looks?
The endless dust-storm of troubles cuts off news and letters;
the frontier passes are perilous, travel nearly impossible.
I have already suffered ten years of turmoil and hardship;
now I am forced to accept a perch on this one peaceful
branch.

Written While Traveling at Night

Sparse grass, a faint wind along the shore,
the tall mast of my solitary boat in the night,
stars hanging low over the flat, wide plains,
moon bobbing up from the great river's waves...
How can a man make a name by writing?
Old age and illness have ended my career.
Drifting, drifting . . . what am I like?
Between heaven and earth, a wind-blown gull.

On Yueyang Tower

Long ago I heard about the waters of Dongting;
at last I have climbed Yueyang Tower to view it.
Wu and Chu, east and west, are split by the lake;
heaven and earth, day and night, float in its waters.
From friends and relatives, not a word of news.
Old and ill, I have nothing but my little boat.
War horses fill the passes to the north.
I lean on the guardrail, sobbing and weeping.

Meeting Li Guinian in the South

At the home of the Prince of Qi, I have often seen you,
and in the hall of Cui Jiu, I have heard you sing.
Truly these southlands boast unrivalled scenery—
to see you once again when the flowers are falling.

Bai Juyi (772–846)

Invitation to Liu Nineteen

I have some unfiltered wine, "green-ant" fresh,
and a little red clay warming-stove.
Evening is falling, and the sky looks about to snow.
Will you drink a cup with me, or no?

Liu Zongyuan (773–819)

Dwelling Beside a Stream

Long tied down by the official hatpin and seal-cord,
now it seems fortunate to be banished to these southern
lands.
I live at leisure here among the farmers' fields,
looking at times like a rustic from the hills.
At dawn the farmers' plows turn the dewy grass,
at night oars clatter in the rocky stream.
Rambling around, I encounter no one;
I sing long songs to the blue skies of Chu.

Li Shangyin (ca. 812–858)

Untitled

It is hard for us to meet, harder still to part;
the east wind cannot halt the flowers' decay.
The spring silkworm spins till death ends his thread;
the candle drips tears till its wick is ash.
At the morning mirror she grieves that her hair will gray;
reciting poems at night, she feels moonlight's chill.
Peng Mountain, home of immortals, is not far away—
may a bluebird tell her how I long to see her!

Night Rains: Lines to Send North

You ask the date of my return; I have no answer.
Pa Mountain's rain swells the autumn pool.
When will we trim the candle together by the west window
and talk of the time rain fell on Pa Mountain?

Liu Yong (987–1053)

A Song of Parting

To the Tune "Yu Lin Ling"

Cicadas unstrung by cold,
and I, facing the traveler's pavilion at sundown
as the sudden rain-shower halts.
In the tent by the capital gate, the farewell party drags on,
and I linger, too,
though the little boat seems eager to leave.
We hold hands, stare into each other's tear-filled eyes,
afraid that if we spoke our frozen sobs would melt,
thinking of parting—
departing into a thousand miles of misty waves,
the evening clouds banked deep in the wide sky of Chu.

Lovers have grieved at parting through all of time;
how can one bear the desolate cold of fall alone?
There's wine for tonight, but waking who knows where—
a willow-covered bank, dawn wind, a faint rind of moon.

Once gone, years may pass,
and what should be lovely times
and gorgeous views become pointless—
even if overwhelmed by romantic feelings,
who could I share them with?

Thoughts of Return

To the Tune "Pasheng Kanchou"

Before me the patter of rain sprinkling evening sky and river
washing the cool autumn once more
a frosty wind gradually rises, chilly and hard
mountains and river grow more desolate
a few last rays of sunlight fall on the balcony
red fading everywhere, green ebbing
nature's glories disappear
only the waters of Long River
flowing silently east.
I can't bear to climb to the high overlook
and gaze far into distance toward my old country
thoughts of return are hard to stop.
I sigh over last year's footprints—
why linger here in such pain?
I imagine my beautiful love
in her dressing-room expectantly lifting her head
how many times, but no—
it's not my boat returning.
How can she know
that I lean on the railing here
filled with frozen sorrow?

Yan Shu (991–1055)

"There Is Nothing One Can Do"

To the Tune "Huan Xi Sha"

Putting new words to an old tune, drinking a cup of wine;
last year's weather, the same pavilion and tower;
the sun sets in the west, but when will it return?
There's nothing one can do, flowers go on falling,
familiar looking swallows come back again.
On the fragrant garden path, I pace up and down alone.

Where Are You Now?

To the Tune "Die Lian Hua"

Chrysanthemums by the fence grieve mist, orchids weep dew;
the silk curtain is chill,
the paired swallows fly away.
The bright moon knows nothing of the bitter sorrow of
parting;
its slanting light falls through the vermilion door till dawn.

Last night's west wind withered the green trees.
Alone, I climb the tall tower,
my eyes follow the road off the edge of the earth.
I'd like to send letters on colored paper and white silk,
but the mountains are tall, the waters wide—
who knows where?

Ouyang Xiu (1007–1072)

First Full Moon

To the Tune "Sheng Zha Zi"

On last year's First Full Moon
lanterns lit the flower-market bright as day.
When the moon reached the willow's top,
just past twilight, I met my love.

On this year's First Full Moon
both moon and lanterns are the same,
but last year's love is nowhere seen.
Tears soak my spring gown's sleeves.

Lyric in the Third Month

To the Tune "Die Lian Hua"

Deep, so deep the courtyard lies, piled
how deep this mist of willows, fold
on fold of gauzy curtains!
His jade bridle, carved saddle, do they wait before the
house of pleasure?
From so high up, I can't see Changtai road.

Rain in torrents, wind raging, this March evening.
I close my door on twilight,
unable to hold onto spring.
Tears in my eyes, I implore the flowers,
but the flowers never speak—
just a red rush past the garden swing.

Alone on the High Balcony

To the Tune "Die Lian Hua"

Alone, on the high balcony,
I lean against the railing in a light breeze,
staring into my dark grief at her leaving now blackening the heavens.
The bright grass on the hillside still clutches the sunlight within it.
Who could know my feelings, leaning here?

Might as well get crazy drunk, I think.
I turn to wine, I turn to song,
but the forced merriment is tasteless.
Gradually, though, my sash loosens—
how can I regret it all? She is a girl worth aching for!

Li Qingzhao (1084–ca. 1151)

Words to the Tune "Tipsy in the Shade of Flowers"

[Zui Hua Yin]

Thick clouds overhead, thin mist below,
they go on forever, these days of sorrow.
In its censer formed like a golden animal,
the borneol incense melts away.
Once again it is the season of the Double Ninth Festival;
I lie on my jade pillow behind thin silk curtains.
Halfway through the night the chill first penetrates.

After dusk I stood by the eastern fence
holding a cup of wine, an elusive fragrance filling my
sleeves.
Don't tell me that I should not be overcome by grief.
My curtains flutter in the west wind,
and I feel as frail as a chrysanthemum.

Words to the Tune "Spring in Wuling"

[Wuling Chun]

The wind dies down, the flowers are all gone,
though the damp earth is still fragrant with fallen petals.
I'm too tired to give my hair its evening grooming.
His things are still here, but he is gone—
everything has ended.
I want to speak of my grief
but tears wash my words away.

They say that in Twin Streams
spring is still lovely,
and I think about going there
to drift in a small boat on the water.
I only fear that these grasshopper boats
that sail upon Twin Streams
cannot support this burden of sorrow.

Yang Guo (ca. 1200–1275)

Lotus Song (1)

The lotus-picking girls
harmonizing their lotus-picking songs
pass beyond the willows
in their little orchid boats,
heedless of the shattered dreams
of mandarin ducks.
How was the night?
All alone I climbed the tower by the river
and lay down there.
When your heart is broken
don't sing the old songs of the southern dynasties.
Bai Juyi's tears were more than enough!

Lotus Song (2)

The boats steer their way home
on the lake where they pick lotus.
A soft wind ruffles
the girls' green silk skirts.
Longing for their lovers' return,
a single tune on the lute
brings many tears.
The lotus flowers finish blooming
and there is still no news.
How cold the evenings are!
Look—those mandarin ducks and white egrets—
is there anywhere they don't fly in pairs?

Guan Hanqing (ca. 1220–ca. 1307)

Sadness at Parting

Ever since we said farewell
my heart has been wrenched by longing.
This lingering need,
when will it end?
Leaning against the railing
my sleeves sweep off
a snowfall of willow catkins.
The stream winds away;
the hill blocks my view.
My love is gone!

Wang Yun (1228–1306)

Country Scene

Words of lotus-pickers lost in autumn haze,
water flat as ribbon.
Neither wind nor light flows away;
they linger together in my hand.
In a painted boat, a smiling face
is still caressed by spring wind.
Though doubtless beautiful,
these mountains and rivers are not my land.
In what day, what season,
what year, will I go home?

Anonymous (Yuan Dynasty, 1234–1368)

The Courtesan's Lament

At the top of the tower
willow tresses toss in the breeze.
The vacant courtyard seems lonely.
Alone, I lean against the railings;
all the peach blossoms are falling.
The green mountains can't tell me
if my love is near or far.

Ma Zhiyuan (1260–1334)

Meditation in Autumn

Withered vines, gnarled trees, twilight crows,
river flowing beneath the little bridge,
past someone's home.
Wind blowing from the west
where the sun sets, blowing
across the ancient road,
across the bony horse,
across the despairing man
who stands at heaven's edge.

Zhang Yanghao (1269–1329)

Retirement Benefits

Removed from office,
I retreat to the country,
abandoning my high ambitions.
Perhaps I *am* unfit,
lazy, undisciplined, not too bright,
since I didn't realize until today
that I don't miss them.
Strolling beside lakes and streams,
sporting in the mountains,
I can go anywhere I like now.
After thirty years of work,
this is what I've earned.
These blue-green hills, strangely enough
seem to share my retirement plans.

Zhang Kejiu (1270–ca. 1349)

Spring Sadness

Still clouded by morning dream, I wake,
feeling as smeared as my rouge.
A little piece of my heart
still blames that young man.
Ten years and no letter
even to say he's all right.
The river bank is green
with turquoise spring grass,
in the apricot village.

Autumn Thoughts

At sky's edge, white geese scrawl characters on cold clouds.
In my green phoenix mirror, a pale, hollow face.
The autumn wind last night blew in gusts of sadness.
I was thinking of you, but couldn't see you.
Singing a melancholy song to myself, I opened my wine jug.
I burned the lamp wick down to a stub,
got half drunk on wine,
that kind of evening.

Autumn Dream

The west wind brought me a letter—
home seems so far away.
They want to know the date
set for my return.
Geese honk in a sky red as autumn,
while down below men get drunk
in a field of yellow flowers.
The sound of rain outside
drumming on banana leaves
brings me this autumn dream.

Liu Zhi (ca. 1280–ca. 1335)

Song of Departure

Warm wind excites swallows and orioles;
sparkling sun makes peach and apricot glow.
The Long River is a smooth shiny ribbon;
evening rain falls in the quiet mountains.
I carry wine for a departure toast,
break off a willow twig for sadness.
I think of that time in Liang Garden.
You're leaving Wei city
when it's full of blossoms.
You've just left the departure pavilion
and I'm already lonely.
I listen sadly
as the Yang Pass Song
is sung for the fourth time.

Guan Yunshi (1286—1324)

Written for Someone

A flight of geese struggles in
fighting the west wind;
I think of the thousand year tragedy
of the Southern Dynasties.
I spread my elegant writing pad
to record deep thoughts.
I've hardly begun
when my brush stops in the air—
my mind gone blank.
Once I could capture time and mood
at one swoop, without error.
Today, weary and miserable,
I have written two vain words
about mutual longing.

Notes on the Poems

Page 33, "A Farewell"
The poem is addressed to his dear friend Meng Haoran, who had just failed the Imperial Examination. Filled with shame, he exiled himself from society.

Page 37, "Drinking Alone Beneath the Moon"
The "far Cloud River" is the Milky Way

Page 40, "Leaving Early for White Emperor City"
This poem celebrates Li Bai's return from exile; at White Emperor City he received news of the Emperor's pardon. The current of the Yangtze River through mountain gorges is very swift, but a thousand miles in a day is likely an exaggeration.

Page 43, "Beside Serpentine Lake"
The First Lady of Zhaoyang palace was Lady Flying Swallow, favorite concubine and later Empress of Han Dynasty Emperor Qeng; Du Fu and other poets commonly substituted her name for that of the current Emperor's concubine Yang Guifei.

This poem takes place during the occupation of Changan by An Lushan's rebel soldiers. Emperor Xuanzong and his court fled the rebel advance through Jiange pass; at Mawei, by the Wei River, the emperor's military escort mutinied and killed Chief Minister Yang Guozhong, the cousin of Yang Guifei, and demanded her death as well; Yang Guifei was strangled. The Emperor is "he who left" and Yang Guifei is "she who stayed"—naturally, they can no longer communicate with each other. Her soul is "tainted with blood" because she was murdered and because she and her family were widely blamed for the revolution.

South is the direction of Du Fu's family; north is the location of the court in exile.

Page 45, "On His Sad Departure from Changan..."
Reference to the belief that a person had ten souls, seven animal and three spiritual, which could be driven from the body by a traumatic experience (such as the bloody occupation of Changan) or severe illness. Rituals were performed to bring them back.

Page 46, "Missing Li Bai at the End of the Earth"
This poem may seem disjointed and hard to follow at first, moving abruptly from swollen rivers to literature, to goblins. Du Fu is riding two trains of thought at once. First, he has not heard from Li Bai since Li was sent into exile, and he worries about the dangers facing him in his travels; he seems particularly concerned about the danger of drowning, which comes up again in both of Du's "Dreaming of Li Bai" poems. Second, he complains that Li Bai has still achieved no security in his life, though he is the greatest poet of his age. Qu Yuan was a fourth century poet, banished by the king of

Chu, who drowned himself in the Miluo River. A later poet, Jia Yi, dropped an offering of poems into the river on his own way to exile.

Page 47, "Dreaming of Li Bai (1)
Souls of the living were believed able to travel at times of unconsciousness, but not as freely as those of the dead.

Page 51, "Welcoming a Guest"
This translation was made for my friend Yo-Hsin Huang.

Page 55, "Passing the Night at Headquarters"
Wutung trees are commonly known as Chinese parasol trees.

After five years with no employment, Du Fu had finally been given a nominal court position by Governor Yen Wu, which would enable him to assume the rights and appurtenances of official rank, and thus a measure of security.

Page 58, "Meeting Li Guinian in the South"
Li Guinian was an extraordinarily fine singer. Favored by Emperor Xuanzong, in whose court he often performed, he became not only famous but wealthy.

Page 63, "A Song of Parting"
The title is my own; poems from this era were given only the titles of the popular tunes to which they had set their words. Since many poems by various poets were set to the same tunes, the titles are not much help in identifying the poems.

Page 71, "Words to the Tune 'Tipsy in the Shade of Flowers'"
The Double Ninth Festival is the ninth day of the ninth month in the lunar calendar. It was celebrated by climbing a hill, drinking wine in which chrysanthemum petals floated, and writing poems.

Page 73, "Lotus Song (1)"
Yang Guo refers to the time (815 CE) when the poet Bai Juyi, having offended the court, was sent away to a provincial post as Marshal in Jiangzhou. The original Chinese here says "the Marshal's tears" but I have substituted the poet's name for clarity.

Page 84, "Song of Departure"
The Yang Pass Song is a parting song which is usually sung three times.

Bibliography of Sources

de Bary, Wm. Theodore; Chan, Wing-tsit; Watson, Burton. *Sources of Chinese Tradition*. New York and London: Columbia University Press, 1960.

Hawkes, David. *A Little Primer of Tu Fu*. Oxford: The Clarendon Press, 1967.

Hucker, Charles O. *China's Imperial Past*. Stanford, California: Stanford University Press, 1975.

Hu Pin-ching. *Li Ch'ing-chao*. New York: Twayne Publishers, Inc., 1966.

Liu, James J. Y. *The Art of Chinese Poetry*. Chicago: Phoenix Books, The University of Chicago Press, 1962.

Liu, James J.Y. *Major Lyricists of the Northern Sung*. Princeton, NJ: Princeton University Press, 1974.

Liu, James J.Y. *The Poetry of Li Shang-yin*. Chicago: The University of Chicago Press, 1969.

Pound, Ezra. *The Translations of Ezra Pound*. New York: New Directions Press, 1953.

Seaton, J. P. *Love & Time: Poems of Ouyang Hsiu*. Port Townsend, Washington: Copper Canyon Press, 1989.

Smith, Bradley & Weng, Wan-go. *China: A History in Art*. New York: Harper & Row, Publishers, Inc., 1973.

Watson, Burton. *The Columbia Book of Chinese Poetry*. New York: Columbia University Press, 1984.

Weinberger, Eliot and Paz, Octavio. *Nineteen Ways of Looking at*

Wang Wei. Mount Kisco, NY and London: Moyer Bell, Ltd., 1987.

Whincup, Gregory. *The Heart of Chinese Poetry.* New York: Anchor Books, Doubleday, 1987.

Yang, Richard F.S. and Metzger, Charles R. *Fifty Songs from the Yuan.* London: George Allen & Unwin, Ltd., 1967.

Yip, Wai-lim. *Chinese Poetry: Major Modes and Genres.* Edited and translated by Wai-lim Yip. Calligraphy by Kuo-syung Chen. Berkeley and Los Angeles: University of California Press, 1976.

Acknowledgments (continued from copyright page)
Feminist Studies: Li Qingzhao, "Words to the tune, 'Spring in Wuling'," "Words to the Tune, 'Tipsy in the Shade of Flowers'."
The Hampden Sydney Poetry Review: Wang Wei, "Seeing Yuan Second Off to An Xi."
Interim: Yan Shu, "Where Are You Now?"
Literary Imagination: Du Fu, "Missing Li Bai at the End of the Earth."
The Literary Review: Xie Lingyun, "Surveying My Fields, I Climb Panxu Mountain at the Mouth of the Sea"; Ma Zhiyuan, "Meditation in Autumn."
Many Mountains Moving: Du Fu, "Meeting Li Guinian in the South."
Northwest Review: Zhang Kejiu, "Spring Sadness," "Autumn Thoughts"; Guan Yunshi, "Written for Someone."
The Pacific Review: Zhang Kejiu, "Autumn Dream."
The Pedestal Magazine: Ouyang Xiu, "To the tune, 'Die Lian Hua' "; Wang Yun, "Country Scene."
Potomac Review: Yan Shu, "There Is Nothing One Can Do."
Renditions: Yang Guo, "Lotus Song (1)," "Lotus Song (2)"; Zhang Yanghao, "Retirement Benefits."
Spoon River Quarterly: Li Bai, "Seeing Meng Haoran Off to Yangzhou"; Meng Haoran, "Poem Sent to Old Friends While Staying Overnight on the Donglu River."
Wordsmith: Du Fu, "Dreaming of Li Bai (1)."

NB: Many of these poems have been revised in preparation for this collection and some appear under different titles.

Companions for the Journey Series

Inspirational work by well-known writers in a small-book format designed to be carried along on your journey through life.

Volume 18

Breaking the Willow

Poems of Parting, Exile, Separation & Return

Translated by David Lunde

978-1-893996-95-3 96 PAGES $14.00

Volume 17

The Secret Gardens of Mogador

Alberto Ruy-Sánchez

Translated by Rhonda Dahl Buchanan

978-1-893996-99-1 240 PAGES $15.00

Volume 16

Majestic Nights

Love Poems of Bengali Women

Translated by Carolyne Wright and co-translators

978-1-893996-93-9 108 PAGES $15.00

Volume 15

Dropping the Bow

Poems from Ancient India

Translated by Andrew Schelling

978-1-893996-96-0 128 PAGES $15.00

Volume 14

White Crane

Love Songs of the Sixth Dali Lama

Translated by Geoffrey R. Waters

1-893996-82-4 86 PAGES $14.00

Volume 13

Haiku Master Buson

Translated by Edith Shiffert and Yuki Sawa

1-893996-81-6 256 PAGES $16.00

Volume 12

The Shape of Light

Prose Pieces by James Wright

1-893996-85-9 96 PAGES $14.00

Volume 11

Simmering Away: Songs from the Kanginshu

Translated by Yasuhiko Moriguchi and David Jenkins

Illustrations by Michael Hofmann

1-893996-49-2 70 PAGES $14.00

Volume 10

Because of the Rain: Korean Zen Poems

Translated by Won-Chung Kim and Christopher Merrill

1-893996-44-1 96 PAGES $14.00

Volume 9

Pilgrim of the Clouds

Poems and Essays from Ming Dynasty China

Translated by Jonathan Chaves

1-893996-39-5 192 PAGES $15.00

Volume 8

The Unswept Path: Contemporary American Haiku

Edited by John Brandi and Dennis Maloney

1-893996-38-7 220 PAGES $15.00

Volume 7

Lotus Moon: The Poetry of Rengetsu

Translated by John Stevens

Afterword by Bonnie Myotai Treace

1-893996-36-0 132 PAGES $14.00

Volume 6

A Zen Forest: Zen Sayings

Translated by Soioku Shigematsu

Preface by Gary Snyder

1-893996-30-1 120 PAGES $14.00

Volume 5

Back Roads to Far Towns: Basho's Travel Journal

Translated by Cid Corman

1-893996-31-X 94 PAGES $13.00

Volume 4

Heaven My Blanket, Earth My Pillow

Poems from Sung Dynasty China by Yang Wan-Li

Translated by Jonathan Chaves

1-893996-29-8 128 PAGES $14.00

Volume 3

10,000 Dawns: The Love Poems of Claire and Yvan Goll

Translated by Thomas Rain Crowe and Nan Watkins

1-893996-27-1 88 PAGES $13.00

Volume 2

There Is No Road: Proverbs by Antonio Machado

Translated by Mary G. Berg and Dennis Maloney

1-893996-66-2 118 PAGES $14.00

Volume I

Wild Ways: Zen Poems of Ikkyu

Translated by John Stevens

1-893996-65-4 152 PAGES $14.00